YouTube®:

How Steve Chen Changed the Way We Watch Videos

WIZARDS OF TECHNOLOGY

WIZARDS OF TECHNOLOGY

YouTube®:

How Steve Chen Changed the Way We Watch Videos

CELICIA SCOTT

Mason Crest

Mason Crest
450 Parkway Drive, Suite D
Broomall, PA 19008
www.masoncrest.com

Printed and bound in the United States of America.

First printing
9 8 7 6 5 4 3 2 1

Series ISBN: 978-1-4222-3178-4
ISBN: 978-1-4222-3188-3
ebook ISBN: 978-1-4222-8724-8

Library of Congress Cataloging-in-Publication Data

Scott, Celicia, 1957-
    YouTube : how Steve Chen changed the way we watch videos / Celicia Scott.
        pages cm. — (Wizards of technology)
    Audience: Age 12 plus.
    Audience: Grades 7 to 8.
    ISBN 978-1-4222-3188-3 (hardback) — ISBN 978-1-4222-3178-4 (series) — ISBN 978-1-4222-8724-8 (ebook) 1. Chen, Steve, 1978-—Juvenile literature. 2. Telecommunications engineers—United States--Biography—Juvenile literature. 3. Computer scientists—United States--Biography--Juvenile literature. 4. YouTube (Electronic resource)—Juvenile literature. 5. Internet videos—Juvenile literature. I. Title. II. Title: You Tube.
    TK5102.56.C44S36 2015
    384.55'8—dc23
                                                2014012234

CONTENTS

KEY ICONS TO LOOK FOR:

 Text-Dependent Questions: These questions send the reader back to the text for more careful attention to the evidence presented there.

 Words to Understand: These words with their easy-to-understand definitions will increase the reader's understanding of the text, while building vocabulary skills.

 Series Glossary of Key Terms: This back-of-the book glossary contains terminology used throughout this series. Words found here increase the reader's ability to read and comprehend higher-level books and articles in this field.

 Research Projects: Readers are pointed toward areas of further inquiry connected to each chapter. Suggestions are provided for projects that encourage deeper research and analysis.

 Sidebars: This boxed material within the main text allows readers to build knowledge, gain insights, explore possibilities, and broaden their perspectives by weaving together additional information to provide realistic and holistic perspectives.

Words to Understand

programming languages: Code for telling a computer what to do, designed to be easily understood by humans.
profitable: Making money.
investment: Money, time, or effort put into a company in the hopes of getting even more back.
stocks: Shares of a company, which can be bought and sold.
acquire: Buy another company and add it to form one larger company.

CHAPTER ONE

Ambition

Steve Chen is an ambitious man. He's full of new ideas, and he has no plans of sitting back and doing nothing any time soon!

YouTube is what Steve is best known for, but it's not the only company with which he has been involved. As a former employee of PayPal and Facebook, he has gone on to play an important role in many other companies after Google took over YouTube. His next project began just a few years later. Like YouTube, it focuses on improving what the Internet has to offer.

Steve Chen and Chad Hurley began AVOS Systems in 2011 along with Vijay Karunamurthy. That same year, Steve Chen was listed as one of the "Fifteen Asian Scientists to Watch" by Asian Scientist Magazine, due to his

Steve Chen's story started on the other side of the world, in Taipei, Taiwan. Taipei is the capital city of the Republic of China, a small island nation with a complicated relationship with the much larger People's Republic of China.

seemingly endless ambition. According to the company's website, AVOS aims to, "help developers create fun and beautiful apps faster than ever." Apps, short for applications, are programs that are used on mobile devices and computers.

Steve has accomplished a lot—but it didn't come easily. He needed to overcome a lot of trials to get to where he is today. His first few years were not spent in the United States, but in Taiwan. In order to succeed, he needed to really push himself outside of his comfort zone. His story proves that amazing success can come out of great determination!

CHILDHOOD

Steve was born on August 18, 1978, in Taipei, Taiwan, and he spent the first few years of his life there. As an adult, he admitted, "I don't remember much from Taiwan." His knowledge of the language and culture of Taiwan is limited. "A lot of what I ended up learning is through trips back there," he said. As an adult, he believes his Chinese language skills are at a first-grade level.

Steve and his family lived in Taiwan until he was eight years old, and then they immigrated to the United States. "The reason why we came to the U.S. was led by my father," Steve explained. According to Steve, his father, who was in the trading business, "was asked to start a branch in New York or Chicago, and he ended up choosing Chicago." The Chen family left Taiwan as Steve was entering second grade.

At the time of Steve's arrival in the United States, he spoke absolutely no English. His father began working at his new office, while his mother stayed home to take care of Steve and his younger brother. Steve did not attend a special school or program for children who did not know English; he was put right into a typical Chicago classroom and forced to learn on his own.

Life in the United States was difficult for Steve at first. His father's choice to live in Chicago made a big difference to Steve's family. If they had lived in a city like New York, for example, they could have joined a large

Chicago is an exciting and vibrant city—but it has a very small Asian American community.

Asian-American community. Chicago, however, had very few people with whom Steve and his family could relate. Steve believes, though, that the challenges he faced as a child ended up being good for him. "It was very valuable having that experience growing up in the Midwest, sort of being the only Asian kid all the way until junior high," he said.

For Steve and his younger brother, home life and school life were drastically different from one another. "There really weren't many Asian influences outside of the house that we lived in," he explained. Despite coming from an uncommon culture, though, Steve said, "My brother and I didn't really feel any different than any of the other kids that were growing up in the Midwest." They were treated as equals.

Steve worked very hard to learn English. Even as a kid, he loved learning about anything new. His favorite subject to read about was technology. He may have felt lonely and different sometimes, but he didn't let that get in the way of his learning.

He finished elementary school and middle school, and then applied to the Illinois Mathematics and Science Academy as a sophomore in high school. This school is very selective; not everyone who applied was able to get in. Steve was one of the lucky few.

The academy was a boarding school, which meant Steve needed to move away from home to attend. He stayed at the academy from the time he was thirteen until he was seventeen and graduated. His school encouraged its students to explore their interests and allowed them to study whatever they liked for one day a week. "The great thing about it was that it was one of the first schools that was plugged into the Internet," he recalled. Having access to computers and the Internet helped Steve develop his love for **programming languages** before he stepped foot in college.

When it came time to go to college, Steve attended the University of Illinois at Urbana-Champaign where he studied computer science. Steve grew up in a time where computers were becoming increasingly common in everyday households. The Internet was just starting to bloom, creating endless possibilities for people who got involved during its early stages.

PayPal's headquarters are in San Jose, California. While Steve worked for PayPal, he met the people who would help him create YouTube.

Part of the reason Steve went to the college where he did is because it had a lot of connections to the academy he attended. According to him, about 60 or 70 percent of the kids from his high school academy went on to study at the University of Illinois. "It was the only school that I applied to," Steve said in an interview. One of the other future founders of YouTube, Jawed Karim, also studied computer science at the same university.

PAYPAL

After college, Steve was immediately drawn to projects that showed promise, but he needed a little extra push to take the leap and leave his college life behind. When a few of his friends had a great idea and asked Steve to join them, it was just the push he needed. "They had moved out to Palo Alto in California and they had started PayPal at the time." Steve said. "They were trying to *recruit* people to help start the company."

Steve was more than interested. Moving from Illinois to California was a very big, life-altering decision, but Steve knew he needed to take that chance. "The toughest challenge was getting my parents to be okay with that decision," he admitted in an interview. After all, he was barely even out of college at that point. Just five days after having a long discussion with one of his future coworkers, Steve decided to make the big leap into a new life. He flew to California and started working at PayPal.

PayPal began as a startup company. Startup companies are just taking off, and they have a lot of room to grow. Unfortunately, startups aren't always *profitable*. It can be many years before they make any money, and all of a startup's employees must work long, hard hours until that happens. Working for one of these companies is an *investment*. If a startup company becomes successful, the early employees will rise with it. If it fails, the early employees will only have their experience as a reward.

Steve's expertise in computer science was what landed him a job at PayPal, a service that was officially launched in 1999. The service allowed users to exchange money quickly and securely over the Internet, something

Chad Hurley was one of the people Steve met when they both worked at PayPal.

Make Connections

Digital video files are not all created or read the same way. There are many different video languages, or codecs, to choose from. To watch these videos, a user will need to download the required codec and install it into a media player. The media player then reads the codec, and is able to display a video that the user can actually watch. It is possible to translate a video from one codec to another, but this was a difficult task for anyone who was not a computer expert until the dawn of YouTube.

that had not existed up until that point. Today, many merchants allow customers to pay them directly using a PayPal account.

Working for PayPal benefited Steve in a few ways. He gained a lot of experience, but the biggest boon from working there was meeting Chad Hurley and Jawed Karim, the two people who would later help him start YouTube. Steve described how he first met Chad: "We had met each other at PayPal early in 1999. He was one of the first designers with PayPal and one of the first engineers. We worked very closely together through the beginning of PayPal as well as through the acquisition by EBay."

PayPal did not exist for very long before it had a potential buyer. In 2002, it was offered as a publicly traded company, which meant that anyone could buy *stocks* and invest in PayPal. EBay, a budding online auction website, saw ways it would benefit from using PayPal. PayPal would make EBay's service even more popular than it already was because customers would be able to pay sellers in a safer, more secure way.

EBay seized the opportunity to *acquire* PayPal and bought the service for $1.5 billion in 2002. This buyout left the previous employees of PayPal

Text-Dependent Questions

1. At what age did Steve leave Taiwan and why did his family decide to leave?
2. How did growing up in Chicago shape Steve's childhood?
3. When did Steve start working for PayPal and what important people did he meet there?
4. What event inspired Steve to invent a website where users could share videos? Explain.
5. Before the invention of YouTube, why were images easy to share while videos were not?

with a lot of money and countless options for how they would spend it. Meanwhile, EBay continued to prosper from the use of PayPal, which became the preferred method of payment for many EBay users.

A NEW VISION

Steve and his former coworkers stayed in touch. "The older-timers with PayPal continued to meet up throughout the Bay Area for dinners," Steve said in an interview. "It was really just a wonderful mix of people." Together, they came up with the idea for YouTube in 2005.

By this point, Steve decided he was going to stay in California. "I had just purchased a place in San Francisco in early 2005," he explained. Steve wanted to share his new home with his friends and former coworkers, so he invited them over to visit. "I was having the first dinner party at my place and we were taking both videos and photos with digital cameras," he said. Little did he know that this party would prompt him to come up with the idea for YouTube!

Research Project

Steve Chen had a lot of help when he first came up with the idea for YouTube. Chad Hurley, Jawed Karim, and Steve Chen became the three cofounders of the company. Using the Internet, research Chad and Jawed to see where they are now. What companies have they joined and invested in since they helped create YouTube?

After the dinner party, Steve and his friends wanted to share with each other the videos and photos they had taken. They could share the photos easily, because image-sharing websites already existed. At the time, Flickr was one of the most popular ones. For those who did not want to use a website, sending photos through e-mail was another option.

Videos, on the other hand, just couldn't be shared easily. "They were too big to e-mail back and forth," Steve explained, but that wasn't the only reason videos were difficult to share. "You had to download different things based on what digital cameras people had," and that was a hassle. There were many different video formats, and each one used a different language, or codec. Without that codec, a movie was unwatchable.

Sharing videos over the Internet seemed to be more trouble than it was worth for the average user, so many people just gave up and didn't try to share their videos. "We really started to see that this was an unmet need, not just recently, but from all the way stretching back to the first videos that were taken," he said. "They were just living on computers and they had no place to upload their videos."

Steve and his friends knew they had a great idea. A website like You-Tube would provide a place for everyone to upload a video with ease.

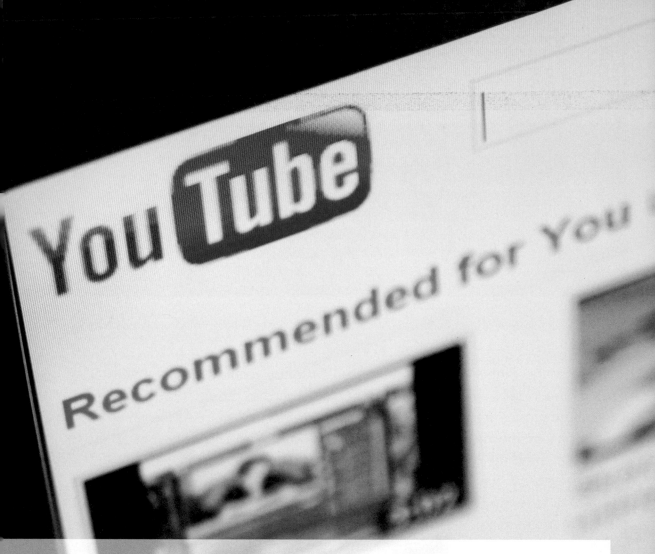

Words to Understand

reliable: Able to be depended on.

domain: The address of a website that you type into your browser.

medium: A way of doing or communicating something.

copyright infringement: Breaking the laws protecting the things people make, such as by selling or displaying art or movies that aren't yours.

monitor: Keep track of.

CHAPTER TWO

YouTube Is Born

All successful companies start with a great idea. Actually putting that plan into action is another story, however. Startup companies need resources such as funding, a place to work, and employees that are willing to work for very little payout until the company can get on its feet. It can be years before startups see a profit, so people working for a startup need to really believe in what they are working for!

Steve found **reliable** cofounders in Chad Hurley and Jawed Karim. They were willing to stick with the company while it was in its beginning stages because of their experience with PayPal. They knew they would be providing a service to the world that wasn't available before they came up with it. Their primary goal was to help the world share videos in a way no one could before. If the three friends could get rich in the process, so much the better!

Chad Hurley was the one who came up with name "YouTube." He also drew the logo.

THE COMPANY BEGINS

With so many different available codecs, a website like YouTube wouldn't be possible without some sort of standard video code. Before YouTube, users who wanted to translate a video from one format to another would need a special program and a lot of knowledge to do so.

Today, every single video that is uploaded to YouTube is automatically translated into a format that Adobe Flash Player can read. Chad explains, "Someone could upload any video format and we could re-encode that in Flash." Anyone who has Adobe Flash Player installed can view any video on the website. With that problem solved, the founders of YouTube could move on to building the website.

Make Connections

The cofounders of YouTube knew exactly what website they wanted to create, but they did not have a name for it yet. They spent time writing down a bunch of names on a list before choosing the right one. According to Steve, it was Chad Hurley who came up with the name and drew the original logo for YouTube: "There was a list of names on the left side, and he ended up drawing the YouTube logo. There was sort of this 'aha!' moment that just said 'Okay, that's it. That's the logo and that's the name we're going with.'"

YouTube.com was officially registered as a ***domain*** in February of 2005, but Steve, Chad, and Jawed still had a lot of work to do. Every website costs money to run, and YouTube would not be cheap. Website owners must pay for the bandwidth that a website uses. Bandwidth is a measurement of the data transferred from the website to a visitor. Many websites pay for the bandwidth their website uses by hosting ads. At first, Steve and his friends did not want to do this.

Steve and his team knew that a video website would require a lot more space and bandwidth than an image-sharing website, simply because of the sheer size of the files being shared. "The amount of CPU computational power it takes to run a service like that is probably the highest out of any other startup that you can run," he explained. They would need a lot more money than other startup companies to get started.

Much of the initial funding for YouTube came from the team's own pockets. "It was really rough for a short while," Steve admitted. He had a lot of credit card debt when YouTube first began, and since he was charging everything to his personal credit card, the debt just kept growing.

The immense pressure to turn a profit helped push them forward. "It's the thing that motivates us to work eighty, ninety hours a week without problems," Steve said.

Fortunately, they didn't have to work that hard for long. The team found some wealthy investors who liked the idea so much that they chose to fund it early on. Startups that receive funding from investors are referred to as angel-funded because of the help they receive from people who are already wealthy.

YouTube did its best to keep its budget small despite the outside help it was getting. Like many famous technology startups, it began in a garage to reduce costs. A public preview of the website was made available in May 2005, pulling in an average of 30,000 visitors to the website per day.

A lot of people began to take notice of YouTube, with Sequoia Capital being one of the first companies to invest money into the project. An initial $3.5 million was invested into YouTube by Sequoia Capital in November of that year, when the website had about 200,000 total registered users. PayPal's chief financial advisor joined YouTube's board of directors at the end of 2005 as well. It was clear by that point that YouTube was getting the attention it deserved. Sequoia Capital eventually invested another $8 million in YouTube. It needed the extra money because of the rising costs of running the website as it became more and more popular.

SHAPED BY THE WORLD

The initial vision for YouTube was very different from what it eventually became. "We thought it was going to be more of a closer circle friendship," Steve said. His team envisioned that people would use YouTube to share videos with friends and family on a smaller scale, with only a handful of people being able to see any one video. "We had no idea it was going to be as big as it was," he admitted.

One of the other ways the cofounders hoped people would use YouTube was alongside PayPal. Videos could be embedded into auction sites like EBay and used as a form of advertising for items being sold.

Make Connections

The founders of YouTube uploaded a few videos before the website was officially public in order to show people how useful the website could be. The first video that was added to the site was one of co-founder Jawed Karim while he was visiting the San Diego Zoo. This video was added on April 23, 2005, and it is still available on YouTube today. Other videos include Steve spending time with his cat and family. At the time, they had no idea so many people would watch and respond to those personal videos!

These videos would give customers a preview of what they were buying before they placed a bid, making both customers and sellers feel more connected. However, for the most part, this was not how YouTube ended up being used.

Rather than force users to see YouTube the way the creators did, they looked at it in another light. "We started building more community features. Along the way, I believe that has helped us be successful. We listen, we observe. We weren't making any assumptions how people were using the site. We would adjust and adapt," Chad explained.

When the website first launched, there was no way to search for videos. The creators hadn't thought there would be a need for a search feature. The way early visitors used the website really surprised the creators. "YouTube isn't an entertainment destination. It's really becoming a site where people come to be informed and to be inspired by video," Chad said. A search function was added once Steve and Chad realized there was a demand for one.

Sharing a unique experience is one of the most important ways people have been using YouTube. "There were these videos that were posted from people from Hurricane Katrina," Steve said. "You see this a lot with

In 2007, Steve was excited to launch YouTube in Taiwan, his birth country.

recent events in which you can search for any of these topics on YouTube and find user-generated content of people that actually live there and are personally impacted by these events, rather than reporters coming and taking video clips."

This sense of connection is not limited to people in the United States. "I hear stories of children in Africa going to computer centers, and going there to watch YouTube. It's inspiring because they're saying that this is

Make Connections

One of the ways YouTube pulled in so many users so quickly was by promising rewards for using the website. In 2005, an iPod Nano was promised to one random user per day until the end of the year, which helped pull in a lot of new users. What kept the users there, however, was how useful and fun the website was!

acting as a window to the world to them. They have a chance to experience cultures beyond their border. They would never have had the opportunity to do that before," Chad said in a 2007 interview.

YouTube has become a way for people to share their unique experiences without a need for an official news outlet. Anyone can upload a video to YouTube, and anyone can come to watch that video with a reliable Internet connection. YouTube has adapted to help people become more connected than ever before. Some of the community features that were added were comments and tags. People who post and watch any video on YouTube can interact with each other, as long as comments are enabled on that video. Messages can even be sent from one user to another.

Some people have said that YouTube is redefining television, but the creators of YouTube do not feel that way. "It's definitely not television. It's a different *medium*," Chad Hurley said. "It's a different experience. People just have a chance to consume video."

GROWTH

Soon, YouTube was considered to be one of the fastest growing websites on the web. In July of 2006, users were uploading more than 65,000 videos each day, and there were 100 million unique views occurring per

Steve and YouTube began to get lots of attention. Here, he and Chad Hurley are being interviewed by the *Wall Street Journal*'s Walter Mossberg.

Make Connections

 How quickly a video loads and can be watched depends entirely on the user's connection with the website. Faster connections can watch videos instantly, while slower connections require buffer time. Videos that are buffering must be partially stored in the computer's temporary memory before they can be watched. As faster connections became more common, YouTube's success began to rise. Users did not need to wait on videos anymore because they would stream instantly. Today, videos can even be streamed directly to a user's mobile device without needing to wait.

day. Two months earlier, YouTube had surpassed CNN.com, a popular news website, in average viewership. By that point, almost half of all videos viewed on the Internet were watched on YouTube. One of the reasons YouTube became so popular so fast is because of the age group it pulled in. Most users of the website were between the ages of twelve and seventeen years old during its first year.

Expanding at such a fast rate put strain on the servers. They needed to be upgraded. This meant that YouTube's creators needed to find a way to make money. Advertising was the best route.

In 2006, YouTube signed a marketing and advertising deal with NBC. In exchange for exclusive access to new content to display on its website, YouTube would display ads for NBC. Likewise, NBC would advertise YouTube and its content in its own way. This was one of the first advertising deals YouTube entered, but it wasn't the only one. CBS, Sony, and Universal Music Group signed agreements with YouTube that same year. (Today YouTube still makes most of its profits off the ads displayed on the site, although the way those ads are displayed has changed over the years.)

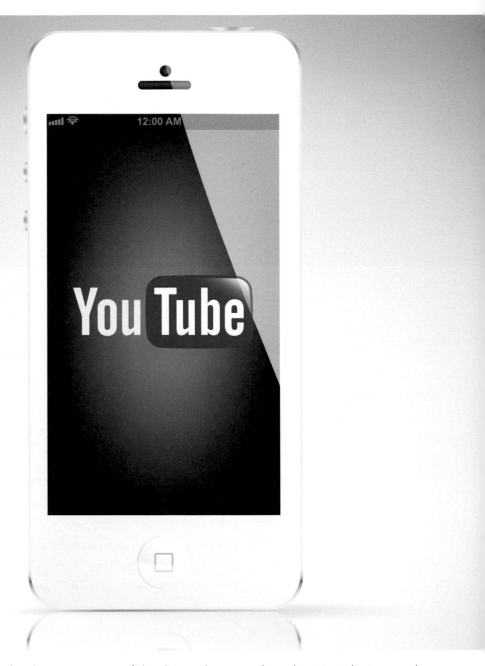

Smartphone technology was one of the things that contributed to YouTube's growth.

According to Steve, many different factors contributed to YouTube's early success. "Broadband penetration in 2005 finally reached the majority of the people in the US and throughout the world," he explained. In other words, more people than ever had access to high-speed Internet and were able to view bandwidth-intensive websites like YouTube from many different locations including home, work, or school.

The video format YouTube chose to use was also widely used at the time. "The video technology that we use is built into Flash," Steve said. Users who already had Adobe Flash Player did not have to download a separate program to use the website. Websites that are easy for visitors to use are likely to grow at a faster rate.

At the same time, more and more people had devices that could record video. Taking videos was no longer restricted to video cameras. Most digital cameras were able to record decent quality video for less than $100. Mobile phones were also rising in popularity, many of which featured picture-taking and video-recording capabilities. All of this fed into the growing stream that was YouTube.

CONCERNS

Steve Chen and his partners had not imagined how fast YouTube would grow. At times, they felt like they were in over their heads. One of the biggest concerns both users and owners had was that YouTube might be used for **copyright infringement**. Copyrighted content, such as music videos, movie clips, or news segments could be uploaded without any real regulation; videos did not need to be approved before they were available for the world to see. The only way to get videos removed was by reporting them so that a moderator could take it down.

A website as large as YouTube could not **monitor** every video that was uploaded. Steve and the other cofounders faced legal action if illegal videos were not taken down in a timely fashion because they were hosted on their website. Throughout YouTube's existence, it has faced

Research Project

The users of YouTube have played a very major role in shaping how YouTube has grown and adapted over the years. Using the Internet, research the history of some features introduced by You-Tube. List a few features that were added and explain how they helped the website become more accessible, then list a few fea-tures that were removed and explain why they were taken away.

many lawsuits from companies and individuals claiming that YouTube does not do enough to prevent copyright infringement.

YouTube has taken many steps to prevent users from breaking the law, but there is only so much the company can do. When users attempt to upload a video, a message is displayed warning them of the rules of the website. These rules need to be agreed to before a video is uploaded. If users break the rules, they can have their accounts suspended and all their content deleted.

On the other hand, YouTube protects user-generated content. Every single video that is uploaded to YouTube, even a home video, is copy-righted by default once it is uploaded. That means YouTube users can't steal and claim that video as their own. "We're trying to create a system that works for everyone. Every single piece of content that's added to our system is copyrighted. When you take a video, it's copyrighted," Chad explained. However, it is up to the person or group being in-fringed upon to make a copyright claim. They can submit this claim to YouTube, who will review the video and then take it down if it is found to be violating any rules.

At first, one of the ways YouTube attempted to prevent situations in which content could be stolen is by limiting how long a video could

Text-Dependent Questions

1. Why did YouTube choose to automatically encode all uploaded videos into a Flash format?
2. How did the creators of YouTube hope the website would be used by its first visitors? How was that different from the way users actually used the site?
3. What were some of the ways YouTube adapted to the ways the first visitors were actually using the website?
4. In what ways has YouTube made the world feel more connected? List two examples.
5. How does YouTube make most of its money?
6. What technological advancements happened around the time YouTube was founded that helped the website grow in popularity?
7. What steps did YouTube take to prevent copyright infringement?

be. "We've limited, really early on, the length of the videos. That's ten minutes in length to cut down on infringement," Chad said in a 2007 interview. The early restrictions placed on YouTube were eventually lifted, however, as the website grew and adapted to the way people were using it. Software was developed to identify copyright infringement long before that video reached the public, protecting both YouTube and victims of that infringement.

And meanwhile, the site just kept growing.

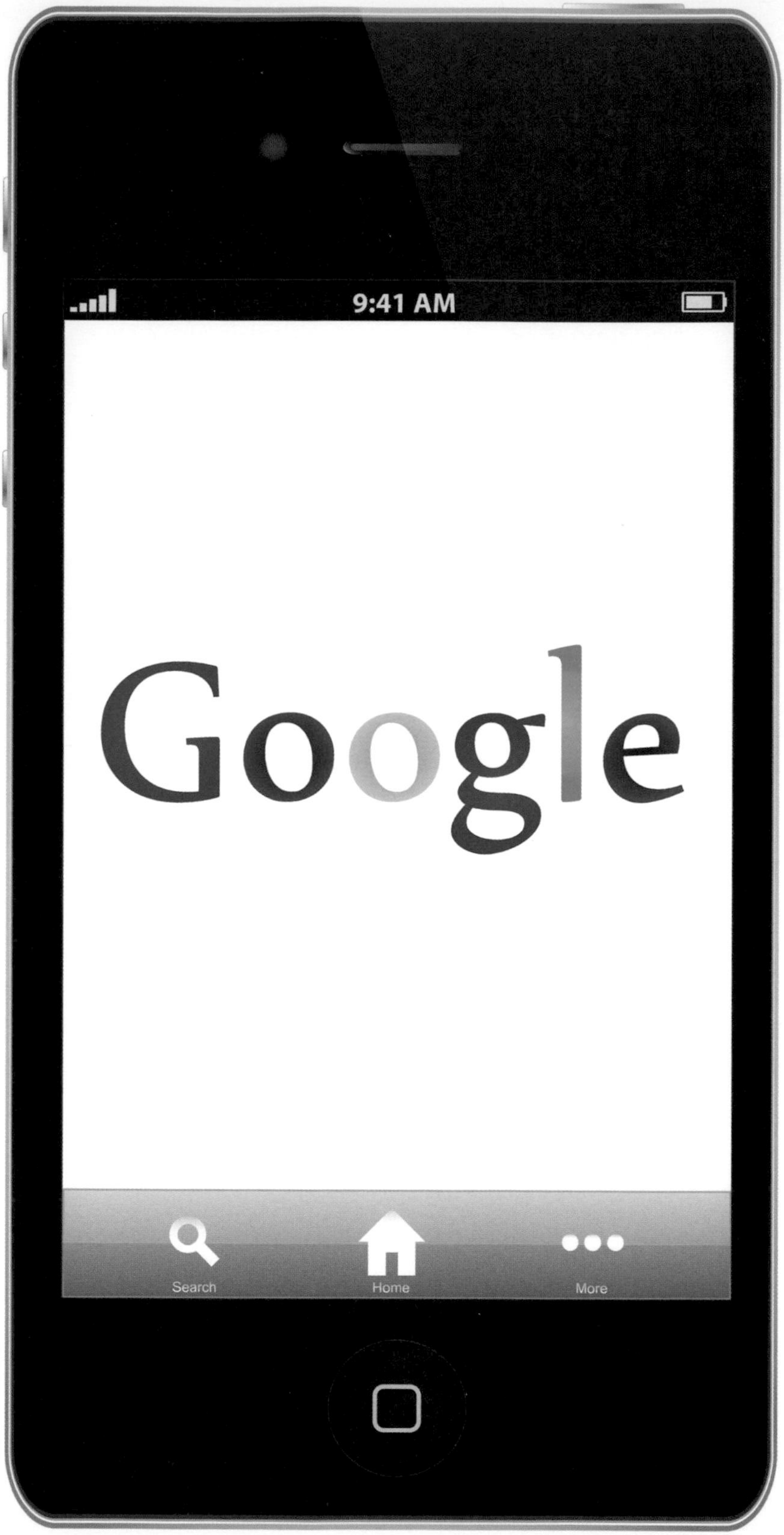
9:41 AM
Google
Search
Home
More

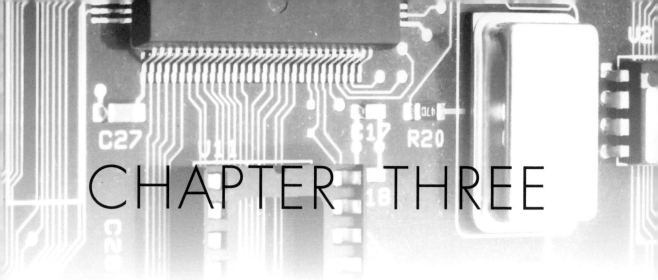

CHAPTER THREE

Working with Google

The threat of potential lawsuits loomed over Steve and Chad's heads. Steve says his team realized, "There was no way we could leverage or hire the resources alone." The problem was just too big for them to handle. They decided they needed to sell their startup to a larger company that would be able to deal with all the problems.

On October 7, 2006, Steve Chen and Chad Hurley uploaded a video for all YouTube users to see. It began with Chad saying, "Today we have some exciting news for you: we've been acquired by Google." Steve continued by thanking the users of YouTube for all their help in reaching this point. "Thanks to every one of you guys that have been contributing

Eric Schmidt, Google's CEO, was convinced that buying YouTube would put Google at the front of a growing "revolution," as more and more people interacted with each other and the world through technology and the Internet.

Make Connections: Person of the Year

Every year, *Time Magazine* picks an influential individual to become its person of the year. The people chosen to become person of the year are often presidents, international leaders, or very important businessmen. In 2006, the cover of *Time* featured a mirror inside of a YouTube screen as its person of the year, signifying that user-created content was very important, and more worthy of recognition than any one individual that year. YouTube was also named Invention of the Year by *Time Magazine* in 2006.

to YouTube, the community. We wouldn't be anywhere close to where we are without the help of this community," he said

The deal with Google was finalized in November. The owners of YouTube received about $1.65 billion worth of Google stock. Its co-founders and employees would now technically work for Google, although they were allowed to continue to develop the website independently. For Steve and Chad, this was the best possible situation. They would get to continue being innovative without the hassle of legal complications.

GOOGLE TAKES OVER

At the time of YouTube's acquisition, it was one of the largest purchases Google ever made. Although YouTube wasn't very profitable yet, the chief executive officer (CEO) of the company believed buying YouTube was a good investment. "This is just the beginning of an Internet video revolution," Eric Schmidt, Google's CEO, said in an interview. Other investors

With Google behind the company, YouTube was able to do much more than it would have been able to without the Internet giant.

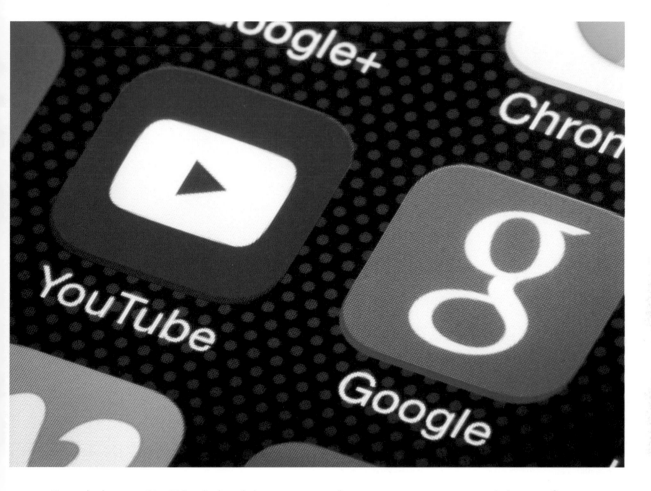

Google buying YouTube helped the company do more to improve its mobile app for smartphones.

in the company clearly agreed because Google's stock price began to rise after the deal was announced.

Some of YouTube's users were concerned that Google would greatly change how YouTube functioned. Steve tried to reassure the users by saying, "The most compelling part of this [acquisition] is being able to really concentrate on features and functionality for the community."

Sumner Redstone, the owner of Viacom, brought a lawsuit against YouTube, saying that videos copyrighted by Viacom had been distributed through YouTube.

YouTube's cofounders did not need to worry about the business aspects of developing YouTube anymore. They could concentrate on being creative instead.

Google, on the other hand, had a lot of legal problems to worry about. In March of 2007, just a few months after Google took over, Viacom International, Inc., sued the company for $1 billion in damages. Viacom International claimed that YouTube, and Google by extension, had broken copyright laws by allowing users to easily upload videos that were already copyrighted by Viacom. The lawsuit lasted many years, but was finally dismissed in 2010. YouTube had proved that it was doing everything it could to abide by copyright laws and was not intentionally allowing users to break those laws. Viacom has tried to appeal this ruling, but has been unsuccessful.

Viacom versus Google was a very important case because it set the standard for what media is allowed on the Internet in the future. The Digital Millennium Copyright Act of 1998 protected Google because it stated that websites could not be sued for copyright infringement as long as they removed copyrighted content when notified of the violation. YouTube has always done its best to abide by the law, both before and after Google bought it.

PARTNER PROGRAM

In May of 2007, YouTube introduced a way for users to make money alongside YouTube. Popular videos were given the option of hosting advertisements that would be displayed before the user video began. For every person who watched these advertisements, the user who uploaded the video would receive a cut of the money YouTube received.

About 45 percent of the money made through advertising goes directly to YouTube, with the other 55 percent going to the person who uploaded the video. In 2013, the average partner earned about $2 per

YouTube's partner program gave users a chance to make money from the advertisements big companies were running on the site.

Make Connections: Jawed Karim

Jawed, one of the cofounders of YouTube, was not happy about the change that forced him to use a Google+ account to post comments on videos. He posted a comment complaining about this on the same account that he had used to upload the very first YouTube video. Then he deleted every single other video he ever uploaded except the first video as a way to show his displeasure. Jawed has had very little to do with YouTube since its acquisition of Google, instead going on to pursue a graduate degree a Stanford University.

1,000 views to any one video. This may seem small at first, but not if the video is receiving hundreds of thousands or even millions of views! Some people producing YouTube videos have been able to quit their jobs because of the money they make through YouTube.

Most of YouTube's money is made through advertising, which is beneficial for everyone involved. YouTube gains money for hosting the videos, the advertisers gain exposure through paying to have their ads played, and users gain money by allowing advertisements to play before their original content. YouTube's Partner Program started out small, but now has more than a million members. Of course, there are certain rules people must follow to earn money this way. They cannot make money from videos that contain any copyrighted material, even if it is free to use, as this would be profiting off of someone else's work.

Advertisements aren't the only way Google makes money from YouTube. Online video rental has become very successful thanks to websites such as Netflix, Hulu, and Amazon. YouTube introduced its own rental service in 2010, and now offers over 6,000 films. These films can be

Google hoped that Google+ would prove to be as successful as Facebook, but that hasn't happened.

Research Project

YouTube helped Google on its rise to success by allowing Google to profit off the most popular online video hosting website. Using the Internet, research the ways in which Google has changed You-Tube over the years. How has Google's influence altered YouTube for better or worse?

watched instantly on a computer using YouTube's website. The cost of each movie rental varies.

MERGING WITH GOOGLE+

Google introduced Google+ in June of 2011 as an attempt to get involved in the social networking scene. Websites like Facebook and Twitter were extremely popular, and the executives of Google hoped people would use a Google+ networking website because of the way it was integrated with so many other platforms. A user's Android phone, Gmail account, and Google+ account could all be linked together.

Although Google owned YouTube and Google+, the two entities were kept separate until November of 2011, when YouTube users were forced to merge their YouTube accounts with a Google+ account, or convert their YouTube account into a Google+ one. This led to very mixed feelings. Google+ users were required to use their real names, while YouTube had been allowed to use a username, or alias, to post on videos. Posting under a real name might prevent some of the hostility that sometimes occurs on the Internet, however, as users would now be more accountable for their words.

YouTube has now taken its place as one of the most successful Internet companies.

Text-Dependent Questions

1. Why did Google buy YouTube and what did the owners of YouTube receive in return?
2. What did Steve say to reassure users after Google bought his company?
3. What sort of problems did Google need to deal with after taking over YouTube?
4. What is the Partner Program and how does it work?
5. In addition to advertising, what is another way YouTube makes money?
6. What happened in June of 2011? Was this decision popular with everyone?

The success of Google+ never reached that of other social networking sites, but Google remains the most visited website on the Internet due to its search function, with YouTube being a close second, followed by Facebook. In 2014, YouTube was estimated to have about one billion unique visitors per month. Facebook had one hundred million less than YouTube. Steve Chen and his friends' big idea has certainly paid off.

Words to Understand

internationalized: Started operating in more than one country.

entrepreneur: A person who starts a new business, or takes risks in business to achieve new things.

CHAPTER FOUR

New Projects

YouTube continues to flourish under Google's ownership, but Steve Chen has moved on. Not only has he started a new company with Chad Hurley, but he has also invested in countless other startup projects he believes could one day be as successful as YouTube is today.

When asked if he had any regrets about selling his first startup, he answered, "I never have any regrets that we sold YouTube to Google." According to him, Google is responsible for YouTube's recent success because a lot of Google's innovations helped YouTube grow. "If we didn't have Google, we would not have a mobile product. If we didn't have Google, we would not have an **internationalized** the YouTube product.

YouTube's headquarters are now in this building in San Bruno, California. The building was originally the corporate headquarters for Gap, the clothing company. YouTube bought the building in 2008.

Make Connections

Steve Chen became a Google employee after Google acquired YouTube, which is how he met his future wife. Park Ji-hyun, now known as Jamie Chen, was working at Google as a Korea product marketing manager when she met Steve. They married in 2009 and moved to Tunbridge Wells in the United Kingdom a year later. They have two children now, one son and one daughter.

If we didn't have Google Search, YouTube would not be doing as well as it's doing to be able to find that piece of content that you're finding," he said.

According to Steve, it would have been impossible for him to accomplish as much as Google did with YouTube, so it made more sense to sell the startup to a larger, more capable company. "All these things, we just couldn't do with the sixty-eight-person team that we had," he concluded. Most of the team were relieved when the company was sold.

Steve believes the next step in YouTube's path will be moving more and more to mobile devices. As smartphones become more common and data plans more affordable, it is becoming much easier to watch YouTube videos on the go. "YouTube itself has always been a perfect dance partner with mobile and for a few reasons. One of them is the type of content that you watch on YouTube," he explained. Most YouTube videos are very short and don't require much time investment at all, making it the perfect way to stay entertained while using a mobile device.

Steven with his wife, Jamie, talk to Kamran Elahian, the chairman and co-founder of Global Catalyst Partners, an international venture firm that has invested in many of the world's leading technology companies.

ReadyForZero

ReadyForZero is one of Steve's latest investments, and something he hopes will use technology to help people change their lives for the better.

INVESTMENTS

All Steve's investments have been technology-based because that is what he cares about most. In 2010, he invested in Crocodoc, RethinkDB, Course Hero, and ReadyForZero. Both Crocodoc and RethinkDB focused on using computer languages in a different way, whether creating a document or a new database. Course Hero, however, was used for educational purposes. The website provides a wealth of resources such as study documents, tutors, flashcards, and even online courses. ReadyForZero is a company that creates software to help people control and reduce their debt.

Steve invested in four more companies in 2011: Hearsay Social, ContextLogic, Road Hero, and Beautylish. Hearsay Social helps financial

Steve and his wife are active supporters of San Francisco's Asian Art Museum.

Make Connections

Steve enjoys being creative when inventing something new on a computer, but he has not forgotten his family's roots. Steve and his wife are very generous supporters of the Asian Art Museum of San Francisco. Jamie was even appointed as one of the trustees of the museum in July 2012.

services connect with clients through social media. ContextLogic created the mobile shopping application known as Wish, which is meant to be fun, relevant, and easy to use. Road Hero makes a mobile application called DriveMeCrazy, which can be used to report drivers' good and bad behavior on the road. Beautylish is a social website meant to spread the word regarding beauty products.

The next year, in 2012, Steve invested in Spool and DramaFever. Spool allows you to save documents, articles, and videos to your computer or mobile device for later viewing. DramaFever categorizes and hosts many different popular television shows from around the world and makes them available with subtitles for anyone to watch.

But Steve wasn't only investing on other companies. He also started up his own new venture.

MOVING FORWARD

Steve and Chad Hurley founded AVOS Systems in 2011. The Internet company focuses mainly on improving mobile and web applications that already exist. It has been used as a base for MixBit (another way to share videos that Steve and Chad created), Delicious, and Wanpai (a Chinese

Steve has worked with Chad Hurley for years on some of the most exciting projects the Internet has ever seen. The two hope that AVOS Systems can be their next big success.

del.icio.us

The original Delicious logo from the company's 2003 founding.

video-sharing app). Delicious, originally founded in 2003 and bought by Yahoo! in 2005, was created as a way to store and share online bookmarks with other people. It was a social networking approach to discovering everything the web has to offer and sharing those discoveries with both strangers and friends. AVOS purchased Delicious in 2011 and has been running the website ever since, although the layout changed quite a bit after the purchase was finalized.

AVOS Systems has acquired other companies, including Tap 11, which has given businesses a way to analyze both social and numerical data. Steve and Chad's new company will likely continue to expand in the future, although they may eventually start a whole new project. Only time will tell!

The people at this busy Chinese Internet café are just a few of the 618 million Internet users in China. Steve Chen hopes to bring at least some of his projects to this huge Internet market.

STEVE AND CHINA

Steve might not have been as successful if his family hadn't moved to the United States when he was a child—but he's never forgotten his roots. Steve was born in Taiwan, but also feels a connection with mainland China. "I really believe in the entrepreneurs inside China," he said in an interview, "and a lot of the innovation that's happening in China, and the speed at which things are happening. I'd love to just come here, tell my story, and encourage other people that are thinking about doing something to do something."

One of the downsides to Steve's relationship with the giant nation is that the Chinese government has blocked YouTube for political reasons. China has its own version of a video-sharing website, known as Youku, which it encourages its citizens to use instead. Although Steve's first creation isn't allowed in China, he hopes his other projects will be allowed. "If YouTube can't be in China, maybe Delicious can be in China," he said.

ADVICE FROM STEVE

Steve has learned a lot over the years as an ***entrepreneur***. Based on his experience, he says, "Even if you fail, the experience is good, and you

Text-Dependent Questions

1. Does Steve have any regrets about selling YouTube to Google? Explain why or why not.
2. List three of the startups Steve has invested over the years and explain what their purposes are.
3. What is the purpose of AVOS Systems?
4. When did AVOS Systems acquire Delicious and what is the website used for?
5. Why does Steve have a complicated relationship with China?

don't have any regrets . . . versus if you always had a great idea and you just never tried it because you thought there was going to be too much competition, I think you'll live in regret." According to him, it is better to try and fail than not try at all.

When young entrepreneurs ask him for advice, his answer is always the same: "Go ahead and do it. Just try it."

FIND OUT MORE

In Books

Dijck, José Van. *The Culture of Connectivity: A Critical History of Social Media*. New York: Oxford University, 2013.

Levy, Steven. *In the Plex: How Google Thinks, Works, and Shapes Our Lives*. New York: Simon & Schuster, 2011.

Sahlin, Doug, and Chris Botello. *YouTube for Dummies*. Hoboken, NJ: Wiley, 2007.

Topper, Hilary. *Everything You Ever Wanted to Know about Social Media, but Were Afraid to Ask*. Bloomington, IN: Iuniverse, 2009.

Wooster, Patricia. *YouTube Founders Steve Chen, Chad Hurley, and Jawed Karim*. Minneapolis, MN: Lerner, 2014.

On the Internet

AVOS
www.AVOS.com

The 22 Key Turning Points in the History of YouTube
www.businessinsider.com/key-turning-points-history-of-youtube-2013-2?op=1

The Youngsters Behind YouTube: The Early Years of Chad Hurley and Steve Chen
www.evancarmichael.com/Famous-Entrepreneurs/1172/The-Youngsters-Behind-YouTube-The-Early-Years-of-Chad-Hurley-and-Steve-Chen.html

YouTube
www.youtube.com

YouTube Cofounder Steve Check Explains What He's Doing with His New Company
www.businessinsider.com/youtube-cofounder-steve-chen-explains-what-hes-doing-with-his-new-company-2012-4

SERIES GLOSSARY OF KEY TERMS

application: A program that runs on a computer or smartphone. People often call these "apps."

bug: A problem with how a program runs.

byte: A unit of information stored on a computer. One byte is equal to eight digits of binary code—that's eight 1s or 0s.

cloud: Data and apps that are stored on the Internet instead of on your own computer or smartphone are said to be "in the cloud."

data: Information stored on a computer.

debug: Find the problems with an app or program and fix them.

device: Your computer, smartphone, or other piece of technology. Devices can often access the Internet and run apps.

digital: Having to do with computers or stored on a computer.

hardware: The physical part of a computer. The hardware is made up of the parts you can see and touch.

memory: Somewhere that a computer stores information that it is using.

media: Short for multimedia, it's the entertainment or information that can be stored on a computer. Examples of media include music, videos, and e-books.

network: More than one computer or device connected together so information can be shared between them.

pixel: A dot of light or color on a digital display. A computer monitor or phone screen has lots of pixels that work together to create an image.

program: A collection of computer code that does a job.

software: Programs that run on a computer.

technology: Something that people invent to make a job easier or do something new.

INDEX

ABOUT THE AUTHOR

Celicia Scott lives in upstate New York. She worked in teaching before starting a second career as a writer.

PICTURE CREDITS

6: Rico Chen
8: Sean Pavone | Dreamstime.com
10: indistinctive - Fotolia.com
12: Sagar Savia
14: World Economic Forum
18: Sebastian Czapnik | Dreamstime.com
20: YouTube
24: Rico Chen
26: Joi Ito
28: Maxmitzu | Dreamstime.com
32: Radub85 | Dreamstime.com
34: Charles Haynes
36: Marcel De Grijs | Dreamstime.com
37: 1000words | Dreamstime.com
38: Featureflash | Dreamstime.com
40: Pressureua | Dreamstime.com
42: Sebastian Czapnik | Dreamstime.com
44: Ajv123ajv | Dreamstime.com
46: AVOS Systems
48: Cool Caesar
50: Joi Ito
51: Ballerina battlearena
52: Eric Broder Van Dyke | Dreamstime.com
54: Joi Ito
55: Delicious
56: Piero Cruciatti | Dreamstime.com